"There will never be a true democracy until every adult, without regard to race, sex, color or creed has his or her own voice in the government."

Carrie Chapman Catt
"Votes for All" November 1, 1917,
NAACP Magazine, THE CRISIS

For Violet, my five-year-old flower.
Ask all the questions. —J. A. S.

For my aunt Carmen, who first acquainted me with women's rights. —U. L.

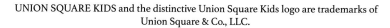

union
square
kids
NEW YORK

UNION SQUARE KIDS and the distinctive Union Square Kids logo are trademarks of
Union Square & Co., LLC.

Union Square & Co., LLC, is a subsidiary of Sterling Publishing Co., Inc.

Text © 2023 Jasmine A. Stirling
Illustrations © 2023 Udayana Lugo

ISBN 978-1-4549-3457-8

Library of Congress Cataloging-in-Publication Data

Names: Stirling, Jasmine, author. | Lugo, Udayana, illustrator.
Title: Dare to Question : Carrie Chapman Catt's voice for the vote / by
  Jasmine A. Stirling ; illustrated by Udayana Lugo.
Description: New York : Union Square Kids, [2023] | Audience: Ages 5-8 |
  Audience: Grades K-1 | Summary: "Carrie Chapman Catt mobilized people
  across the nation to dare to question a woman's right to vote"--
  Provided by publisher.
Identifiers: LCCN 2022025048 | ISBN 9781454934578 (hardcover)
Subjects: LCSH: Catt, Carrie Chapman, 1859-1947. | Suffragists--United
  States--Biography--Juvenile literature. | Women--Political
  activity--United States--Biography--Juvenile literature. | BISAC:
  JUVENILE NONFICTION / Biography & Autobiography / Women |
  JUVENILE NONFICTION / Social Science / Politics & Government
Classification: LCC HQ1413.C3 S74 2023 | DDC 324.6/23092
  [B]--dc23/eng/20220610
LC record available at https://lccn.loc.gov/2022025048

For information about custom editions, special sales, and premium purchases,
please contact specialsales@unionsquareandco.com.

Printed in Malaysia

Lot #:
2 4 6 8 10 9 7 5 3 1
03/23

unionsquareandco.com

Design by Julie Robine

Photo: "About Carrie Chapman Catt" courtesy of Wikimedia Commons.

DARE to QUESTION

CARRIE CHAPMAN CATT'S VOICE for the VOTE

by Jasmine A. Stirling

Illustrated by Udayana Lugo

union
square
kids

NEW YORK

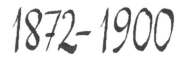
1872-1900

Young Carrie asked too many questions.

She wanted to know how many stars were in the sky,
    if germs had personalities,
        and how long it would take snake eggs to hatch
        behind her mama's oven.

She wanted to know why her daddy was going out to vote,
but Mama was staying home on the farm.

Her daddy threw the eggs in the fire and laughed at her questions.

Especially the last one.

Carrie looked for answers in books but ended up with more questions.

She discovered that in much of the nation,
 women couldn't vote,
  hold office,
   serve on a jury,
    or work in most professions.

In many states, a wife was not allowed
to own property, enter contracts,
or be the guardian of her children.

The truth sank into Carrie's bones.

Carrie's father believed girls didn't need higher education.
So, Carrie—the only woman in her class—
washed dishes to put herself through college.

She wondered:
How does change happen?

She thought maybe cultures changed
the same way living things evolved:
slowly, with lots of small steps.

The way giraffes came to have those
      long,
          long
             necks.

But in society, people had to take those steps
for change to come about.

There was one thing Carrie was certain about.

Voting was essential to the
     beat
        beat
           beating heart of the nation.

After college, Carrie joined the fight for suffrage—women's right to vote.
She vowed to dedicate her life to making women *safe* and *respected*.

VOTES for WOMEN !

Yellow pins, ribbons, and roses united the suffragists under the banner of freedom and equality for all.

Women like Susan B. Anthony taught Carrie all they knew about how to bring about change.

Carrie soaked it up.

She gave speeches by firelight
on the tumbleweed plains of South Dakota.

She screamed down a mountain in a runaway handcar
to get to a rally in Colorado.

She toured the South,
where White women reformers wanted the vote—
but excluded Black women from The Cause.

And she watched as her fellow suffs—
a few determined women who lived for
the movement—failed.

Again and again.

So Carrie dared to question the suffrage movement, too.

She wondered:
Instead of attracting rebels on the fringe,
why couldn't The Cause appeal to
        mothers
                and shopgirls
                        and teachers
                                and ladies who lunch?

Instead of being fueled by a few famous leaders,
why couldn't they recruit millions—
each taking small steps toward change?

And not only that, but—
why couldn't fighting for suffrage be
creative,
celebratory,
and fun?

Susan B. Anthony admired Carrie's daring questions.
In 1900, Susan asked Carrie to step into her role
as leader of the movement.

1900-1920

Carrie knew that to attract mothers and shopgirls
and teachers and ladies who lunch,
she needed to be relatable

        and respectable

                and safe.

Carrie had loved and lost two husbands.
Now she loved a woman.
Mary Garrett Hay—"Mollie Brown Eyes," as Carrie called her—
was Carrie's confidante, strategist, and partner for life. Carrie
kept their relationship—and her most radical ideas—private.

But there was one thing
Carrie didn't keep private:
Her belief that all women
deserved the vote.

Carrie and Mollie knew that they needed a grand campaign
to shake up the country.

Something bigger,
      more spectacular,
            more outrageous,
                  and more, well . . . *fun*
than any campaign, for any movement,
in the history of the nation—if not the world.

A campaign that would make suffrage
as enticing as a chocolate bar.
A campaign that would make it impossible
for the deniers to say
that women didn't want the vote.

Out with the dour and stern.
Out with the grim and gray.
In with suffrage sundaes,

cheerful gals flipping griddle cakes,

ball games, boxing matches,

sandwich boards and socialites.

Carrie and Mollie took on New York—
the most important state in the Union—
with wildly creative campaigns
and a close-knit community
that made suffrage *the thing*
everyone wanted to be a part of.

There were bonfires and fireworks and sing-alongs,
    parties in bejeweled ballrooms,
        and dancing on the streets of
            Harlem, Red Hook, and Little Syria.

The suffs performed plays, wrote music, and wore
costumes for marches that went on for miles.

Hundreds of thousands of women
answered Carrie's call to take small,
everyday steps toward change.

Mothers and shopgirls
and teachers and ladies who lunch
questioned the boxes they had been placed in
and began to climb out.

In November of 1915, the men of New York state took a vote
to say YES or NO to votes for women.

The suffs planned for victory.

Weary and worn, Carrie read the returns to her team by lamplight.
In a cool, steady voice, she gave the news.

They had lost.

"How long will it delay your fight?" someone asked.

"Only until we can get a little sleep," Carrie replied.
"Our campaign will be on again tomorrow morning—
and forever until we get the vote."

Then the Great War came.

Mothers sent their sons off to fight for democracy—
for the rights of free people
to have a voice in their own government—
while women remained banned from voting at home.

Mollie and Carrie didn't believe in war,
but Carrie's commitment to The Cause came first.

She marshaled her army of more than two million suffs
to take on jobs that no women had done before.
They became postmen and porters,
signalmen and shipbuilders.

From dawn to dusk they
worked in factories,
making switches and suits,
tanks and trucks.

Carrie wanted the world to question
what women could do.
She wanted the president
to notice.

President Wilson—a man who believed women belonged in the home and *not* at the polls— was grateful to Carrie.

Women were helping him win the war.
He wouldn't forget.

The men of New York remembered, too.
How could they forget when their wives, sisters, cousins, and mothers were out every night stumping for suffrage!

In November of 1917, those men voted YES,
and gave New York's women the vote.

"THE WOMAN'S HOUR HAS STRUCK!"

proclaimed Carrie, triumphant, with eyes flashing.

"To see her," remarked one listener,
    "was like looking at sheer marble, flame-lit."

Finally, after seventy years of struggle,
countless close misses,
and a great deal of prodding by President Wilson—
the moment came.

On June 4, 1919, the United States Congress passed the Nineteenth
Amendment, granting all American women the right to vote.

There was just one problem.
For the amendment to become law,
thirty-six states needed to agree.
Wisconsin, Illinois, and Michigan immediately said YES!

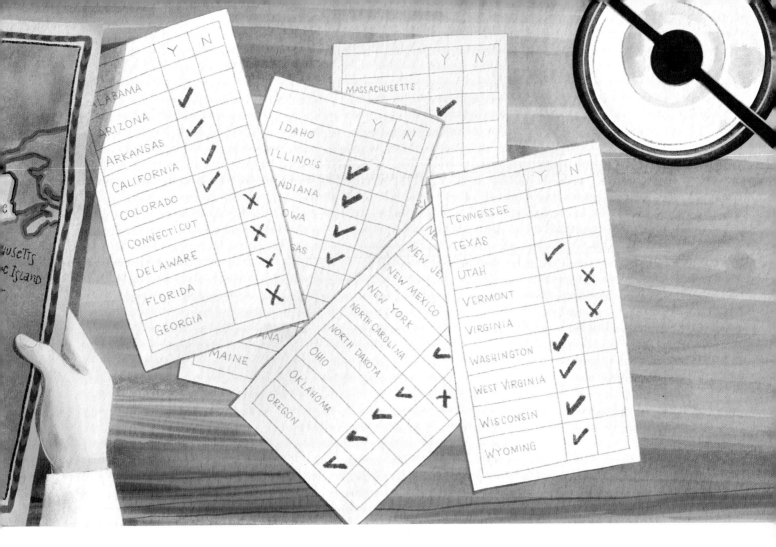

State after state came on board.

    Six states,

        seventeen,

            thirty-five states agreed.

But the rest of the states were stalling, or against.
The amendment was stuck.
Until one seemed like it might go in either direction.
Tennessee.

It would all be decided in Nashville.

1920

Hundreds of people descended on Nashville in August of 1920.
Journalists and lobbyists, businessmen and politicians
streamed into the glamorous Hermitage Hotel.

In the foyer, ladies cooled themselves with palm leaf fans.
Men paced, dripping sweat on marble floors.

Everyone wore roses. Yellow if they believed in votes for women.
Red if they did not.

A hush fell as Carrie Chapman Catt
swept through the front door.
    She carried an overnight bag.
        She sized up the opposition.

She would stay for more than a month.

On the second floor of the Hermitage, the female antis launched their attack.

They claimed voting would make women
bad wives and mothers.

They called Carrie names
and sent her hate-filled letters.

They insisted that if Black women voted,
there would be riots, mayhem,
and blood in the streets.

"The opposition of every sort is here fighting with no scruple, desperately . . ." Carrie wrote to a friend.

The suffs hit the streets.

They visited lawmakers in their homes,
    offices, and hotels.

They kept watch at the train station day and night,
    keeping their allies in Nashville.

They descended on the capitol
    like bees swarming a hive.

Men who started out wearing red roses
changed to yellow. Others switched from
yellow to red. Nobody knew how the vote
would turn out.

In room 309,
Carrie's questions came back.
*How can we get every supporter
to do their part in this fight?*

The muggy heat pressed in on the crowds
as they made their way for the final vote.

Carrie pinned a yellow rose to her dress
with heavy hands.
They did not have the votes to win
and she knew it.

Ninety-six lawmakers settled into their seats,
as the suffs counted roses from the gallery above.

One, two, three, four . . .
48 yellow.
48 red.

We've lost,
  we've lost,
    we've lost.

The clerk called roll.
One by one, all those men cast their votes.

Among them sat a young man,
a representative from the farm town of Mouse Creek.

The clerk said, "Mr. Harry T. Burn."

In the stillness, he stood
with a red rose pinned to his lapel.
He would vote NAY.
That's what the voters in Mouse Creek wanted.

But in his pocket was a letter from his mother, Febb.
It had arrived that morning.

Hon. H. T. Burn
Nashville
Tenn
State Capitol

It was an ordinary letter from mother to son,
about rainy weather,
a little boy's broken arm,
and a neighbor's upcoming wedding.

But tucked into all those details,
was a pointed, motherly question:

Hurrah and vote for Suffrage!
And don't keep them in doubt...
I've been watching to see
how you stood but have not
seen anything yet...
Have you been doing
any serious thinking?...
With lots of love,
Mama

Febb had followed every step of Carrie's career.
She vowed to do what she could—however small—
to win the vote for women.

Harry's heart
      beat
            beat
                  beat beneath his red-red rose.

He clutched his desk.
He cleared his throat.
Quietly, he said,
"Aye."

In the balcony, a confused silence fell.

Slowly, they realized the man from Mouse Creek
had questioned his choice
and changed his vote.

Happy tears wet suffs' faces.
Yellow rose petals fluttered through the air.

Carrie's heart
     beat
          beat
               beat with relief and exhaustion and gratitude.

Silently, she let the news sink into her bones.

On August 27, 1920

Mollie, pale and breathless,
met Carrie on the platform at Penn Station.

The couple of twenty-five years
made their happy way,
amid flashing bulbs and mobs of dignitaries,
to New York's last magnificent suffrage parade.

Great crowds showered them with golden flowers.

Carrie's daring questions
had reinvented a movement,
motivated millions,
prodded a president,
and inspired a letter
that changed a vote—
giving millions of women
the right to cast their own.

AUTHOR'S NOTE

While listening to the radio one day, I was stunned to learn that twenty-seven million American women won the right to vote by a single "aye," changed from a "nay" after a lawmaker received a letter from his mother. A woman I'd never heard of, Carrie Chapman Catt, had been the force behind the vast campaign that led to that single vote.

The spark for this book was lit. I spent several years researching Carrie's life, pouring over her letters at the Library of Congress, getting photos of her room from the historian at the Hermitage Hotel, consulting Black suffrage scholars, studying queer history, and tracking down and collaborating with a descendent of Harry T. Burn.

I faced hard stories about the suffrage movement, too: how White suffragists often excluded Black women, made non-White activists march at the back of parades, and spoke inclusively to some groups and exclusively with others. I grappled with the reality that although all adult citizens were granted the right to vote in 1920, that right was, and still is, often denied to many U.S. citizens.

Carrie dedicated her life to the idea that change comes when everyday people question the status quo and take small steps toward making the world more just and free. Febb Burn's letter shows how one simple act can change the course of history. We all have a role to play in protecting, nurturing, and participating in our democracy. I hope you will follow in Carrie's footsteps. Dare to question!

—J. A. S.

ABOUT CARRIE CHAPMAN CATT

Carrie Chapman Catt, born on January 9, 1859, in Ripon, Wisconsin, dedicated her life to making women safe and respected. Along the way, she successfully campaigned to allow women to enter debates at her college, became the first female superintendent of schools in Mason City, Iowa, and the first female reporter in San Francisco.

Carrie was a tireless leader and a brilliant strategist. As president of the National Woman Suffrage Association, she ignited a movement, expanding the organization to over two million volunteers. Carrie led the cause to victory in 1920, when the Nineteenth Amendment was ratified. Carrie's success was spurred along by many women, including the brave work of Alice Paul and the "Silent Sentinels," who staged months of protests in front of the White House. These women were jailed and mistreated for speaking up.

Carrie remained active in fighting racial, ethnic, and gender discrimination throughout her life. She founded the League of Women Voters in 1920, was featured on the cover of *Time* magazine in 1926, and was the first woman to receive the American Hebrew Medal in 1933. Carrie was featured on a U.S. postage stamp in 1948.

When Carrie died at age eighty-eight on March 9, 1947, she chose to be buried next to her longtime partner Mollie Garrett Hay. They lie under a monument that reads:

HERE LIE TWO UNITED IN FRIENDSHIP
FOR THIRTY-EIGHT YEARS THROUGH
CONSTANT SERVICE TO A GREAT CAUSE

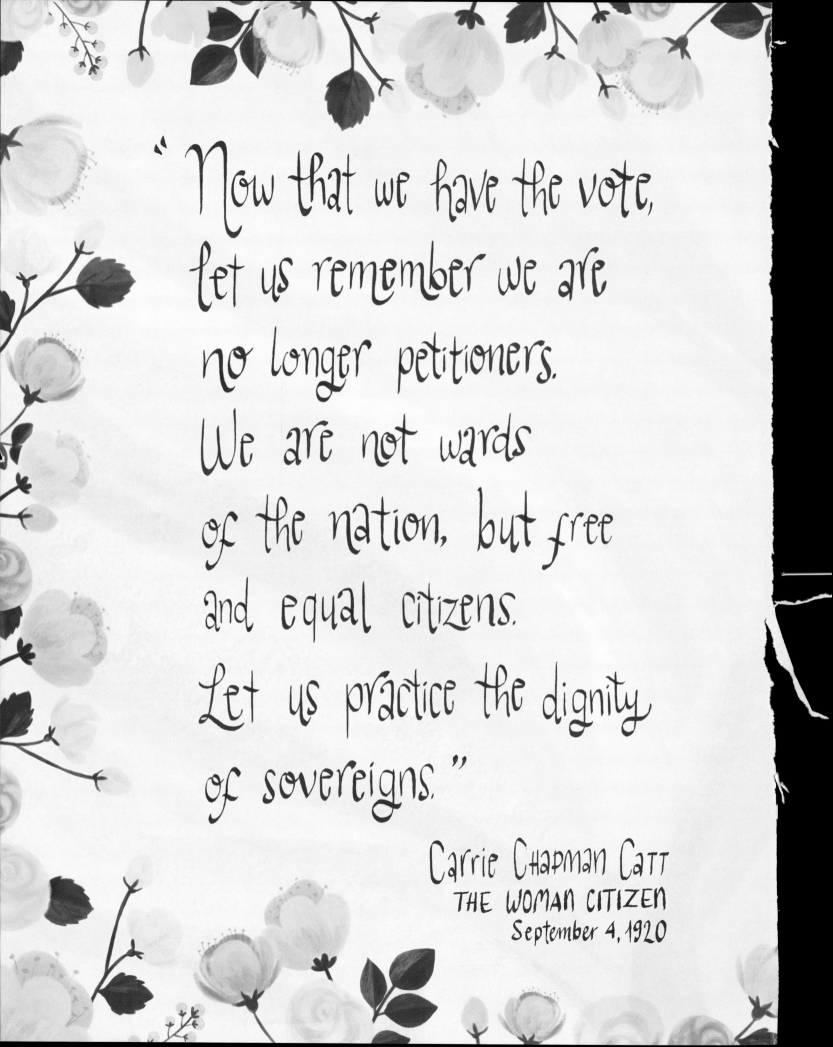

"Now that we have the vote, let us remember we are no longer petitioners. We are not wards of the nation, but free and equal citizens. Let us practice the dignity of sovereigns."

Carrie Chapman Catt
THE WOMAN CITIZEN
September 4, 1920